SUN TZU'S
ART
OF
WAR

SUN TZU'S

ART

OF

WAR

Edited by
Khoo Kheng-Hor
Translated by
Hwang Chung-Mei

Pelanduk
Publications

Published by
Pelanduk Publications (M) Sdn. Bhd.,
24 Jalan 20/16A, 46300 Petaling Jaya,
Selangor Darul Ehsan, Malaysia.

All correspondence to:
Pelanduk Publications (M) Sdn. Bhd.,
P.O. Box 8265, 46785 Kelana Jaya,
Selangor Darul Ehsan, Malaysia.

ISBN 967-978-404-5

1st printing 1992
2nd printing 1994
3rd printing 1995
4th printing 1996

Printed by
Eagle Trading Sdn. Bhd.

PREFACE

*A*lthough Sun Tzu's *Art Of War* is reputed to be the oldest military treatise among the Chinese classical works, and the best and favourite military treatise of all time, it is surprisingly a very small book—it contains only about six thousand Chinese literary characters. There are altogether thirteen chapters in the book, the longest being the eleventh chapter and the shortest, the eigth chapter.

Top world leaders, military strategists, businesspersons and top executives have been obsessed with Sun Tzu's work for years. It is because if one is creative or innovative enough the principles in the *Art Of War* may be applied in limitless ways in every facet of one's life as the Chinese say, *chien pien, wan hua,* that is, a thousand changes, ten thousand forms.

However, it has been rather embarrassing that despite being the 'legitimate heir' to such a great treasure, Chinese business executives are not renowned for their management skills—unlike their Japanese counterparts. This is mainly because the Chinese have not been paying sufficient attention to the *Art Of War*, whilst it is a 'must read' for most Japanese executives.

It is with the hope of making this ancient wisdom accessible to the English-speaking world, especially those English-educated Chinese, that this book is published.

Khoo Kheng-Hor
Hwang Chung-Mei

CONTENTS

INTRODUCTION

*W*hen Sun Tzu, a native of Qi, wrote the *Art of War* some 2,500 years ago, He Lu, the Prince of Wu at that time, was so impressed by what he read that he granted him an audience.

Prince He Lu, who had read all of Sun Tzu's thirteen chapters on warfare, wanted to test Sun Tzu's skill in drilling troops, using women. Sun Tzu was prepared to face this challenge and Prince He Lu sent for 180 ladies from his palace.

Sun Tzu divided them into two companies, each headed by one of the Prince's two favourite concubines. After arming all the women with spears, Sun Tzu asked: "Do you know what is front and back, right and left?"

When all the women replied in the affirmative, Sun Tzu went on to instruct them thus: "When I command 'front', you must face directly ahead; 'turn left', you must face to your left; 'turn right', you must face to your right; 'back', you must turn right around towards your back."

As all the women assented, Sun Tzu laid out the executioner's weapons to show his serious-

"Commands which are vague and not thoroughly understood would be the commander's fault. But when the commands are clear and the soldiers nonetheless do not carry them out, then it is the fault of the officers."

ness regarding discipline, and began the drill to the sounds of drumbeats and shouts of commands. None of the women moved. Instead, they burst into laughter.

Sun Tzu patiently told them that commands which are vague and, therefore, not thoroughly understood would be the commander's fault, and proceeded to instruct them once more.

When the drums were beaten a second time and the commands repeated, the women again burst into fits of laughter. This time Sun Tzu said: "Commands which are vague and not thoroughly understood would be the commander's fault. But when the commands are clear and the soldiers nonetheless do not carry them out, then it is the fault of their officers." So saying, he ordered both the leading concubines out for execution.

The Prince, who was witnessing the drill from a raised pavilion, on seeing his favourite concubines being sent out for execution, was greatly alarmed and quickly sent an aide to Sun Tzu with the message: "I believe the general is capable of drilling troops. Without these two concubines, my food and drink will be tasteless. It is my desire that they be spared."

Sun Tzu replied that having received the royal commission to lead the troops in the field, he can disregard any of the Ruler's commands as he sees fit. Accordingly, he had the two concubines beheaded as an example and thereafter appointed two women next in line to replace the executed ones as company leaders.

Subsequently, the drill proceeded smoothly with every woman turning left, right, front or back; kneeling or rising, with perfect accuracy and precision, without uttering any dissent. Sun Tzu then sent a messenger to the Prince requesting him to inspect the troops which he declared as having been properly drilled and disciplined, and prepared even to go through fire and water for the Prince.

When the Prince declined, Sun Tzu remarked: "The Prince is only fond of words which he cannot put into practice."

Greatly ashamed by what he had heard, and recognizing Sun Tzu's ability, Prince He Lu promptly appointed Sun Tzu as the supreme commander of the Wu armies.

From 506B.C., Sun Tzu led five expeditions against the State of Chu which had regarded Wu as a vassal. He defeated the armies of Chu and forced his way into the Chu capital, Yingdu, while King Zhao fled leaving his country on the verge of extermination.

For almost 20 years thereafter, the armies of Wu continued to be victorious against those of its neighbours, the States of Qi, Qin and Yue. However, after Sun Tzu's death, his successors failed to follow his precepts and suffered defeat after defeat until 473B.C. when the kingdom became extinct.

One

PLANNING

*T*he art of war is of vital importance to the state; the way of life or death; the road to safety or ruin.

It is essential that it be studied seriously. Therefore, appraise it in terms of the five fundamental factors and compare the seven elements later named so that you may assess its importance.

The first of these factors is the Moral Law; the second, Heaven; the third, Earth; the fourth, Command; and the fifth, Doctrine.

By Moral Law, I mean that which causes the people to be in total accord with their ruler, so that they will follow him in life and unto death without fear for their lives and undaunted by any peril.

By Heaven, I mean the working of natural forces; the effects of winter's cold and summer's heat and the conduct of military operations according to the seasons.

By Earth, I mean whether the distances are great or short, whether the ground is easy or

"All warfare is based on deception. Therefore, when capable, pretend to be incapable; when active, inactive; when near, make the enemy believe that you are far away; when far away, that you are near."

"*Hold out baits to lure the enemy; feign disorder and strike him. When he has the advantageous position, prepare against him; when he is strong, avoid him. If he is prone to choleric temper, irritate him.*"

difficult to travel on, whether it is open ground or narrow passes, and the chances of life or death.

By Command, I mean the general's stand for the virtues of wisdom, sincerity, benevolence, courage and strictness.

By Doctrine, I mean the way the army is organized in its proper subdivisions, the gradations of ranks among the officers, the maintenance of supply routes and the control of provisioning for the army.

There is no general who is unfamiliar with these five matters. Those who master them will win; those who do not will fail.

Therefore, when laying your plans, compare the following elements and appraise them carefully: Which ruler possesses the Moral Law; whose commander is the most capable; which army obtains the advantages of Heaven and the Earth; on which side are regulations and instructions carried out better; which army is stronger; which has the better trained officers and men; and in which army is there certainty of rewards and punishments being dispensed with. From these, I will be able to forecast which side will be victorious and which defeated.

A general who accepts my advice should be employed for he is certain to gain victory. A general who rejects my advice will meet defeat, and should be dismissed.

Once my beneficial advice is understood and followed, it will lay the foundation for the knowledge of war. Whenever any extraordinary problem arises, the knowledge gained will help to solve it. But this solid foundation should allow flexibility for one's advantage.

All warfare is based on deception. Therefore, when capable, pretend to be incapable; when active, inactive; when near, make the enemy believe that you are far away; when far away, that you are near. Hold out baits to lure the enemy; feign disorder and strike him. When he has the advantageous position, prepare against him; when he is strong, avoid him. If he is prone to choleric temper, irritate him. Pretend weakness so that he may become arrogant. If he is at ease, put him under a strain to wear him down. When his forces are united, divide them. Attack where he is unprepared; appear where you are least expected.

These are tactics used by a military strategist for victory and they cannot be taught in advance.

One who foresees victory before a battle, will most probably win. One who predicts not much of a chance of winning before the fight, will most probably not win.

More planning shall give greater possibility of victory while less planning, lesser possibility of victory. So how about those without planning? By this measure, I can clearly foresee victory or defeat.

"More planning shall give greater possibility of victory while less planning, lesser possibility of victory. So how about those without planning?"

Two

WAGING WAR

*O*perations of war shall normally require a thousand swift chariots, a thousand leather-covered wagons for carrying stores and a hundred thousand armoured troops, with food supplies transported over a thousand *li* (one *li* is approximately 0.35 mile).

Thus, the expenditure at home and along the way, for fees of advisers and visitors, materials for repairs and maintenance, chariots and armour, may sum up to a thousand pieces of gold a day. Only then can an army of a hundred thousand soldiers be raised.

Victory is the main object in war. If this is long delayed, weapons will become blunt and the ardour of the soldiers will be dampened.

When troops attack cities, their strength will be exhausted, and if the campaign is protracted, the resources of the State will not be enough to last the strain. When your weapons are dulled, your ardour dampened, your strength exhausted and treasure spent, other rulers will take advantage of your extremity to act. And

"Victory is the main object in war. If this is long delayed, weapons will become blunt and the ardour of the soldiers will be dampened."

"Thus, while we have heard of stupid haste in war, we have not yet seen a clever operation that was prolonged. History has shown that there has never been a country benefiting from prolonged warfare."

then no man, however wise, will be able to avert the inevitable that follows.

Thus, while we have heard of stupid haste in war, we have not yet seen a clever operation that was prolonged. History has shown that there has never been a country benefiting from prolonged warfare.

Therefore, one who does not thoroughly understand the calamity of war shall not be able to thoroughly comprehend the advantage going to war.

The skilful general neither requires a second levy of conscripts nor more than one provision. They carry war materials from the homeland, but forage on the enemy. Thus, the army is plentifully provided with food.

When the treasury is impoverished, it is because military operations are being maintained from a distance; carriage of supplies for great distances renders the people destitute.

In the vicinity of the battle, things shall be extremely expensive. When the cost of living rises, the people will sink into poverty and then the government has to use force to collect taxes, thus exhausting the State's strength and finance.

The big battlefield shall become an empty shell with the peasantry losing seven-tenths of their property, while the government will incur expenditures for broken chariots, wornout horses, armours, arrows, crossbows, shields and supply wagons, amounting to six-tenths of its total revenue.

Hence, the wise general sees to it that his troops feed on the enemy, for one cartload of the enemy's provisions is equivalent to twenty of his; one picul of enemy fodder to twenty from one's own store.

To kill the enemy is only out of impulsive rage; but to profit from his defeat is to gain over his wealth.

In battle, those who capture more than ten chariots from the enemy should be rewarded. Change the enemy's flags with our own, mix the captured chariots with ours for our use.

Be kind towards captives and care for them. This is called "using the captured foe to strengthen one's own force."

In war, what matters is victory, not prolonged campaigns. And therefore the general who understands war is the arbiter of the people's fate, and on him depends whether the nation shall be at peace or in danger.

"In war, what matters is victory, not prolonged campaigns. And therefore the general who understands war is the arbiter of the people's fate, and on him depends whether the nation shall be at peace or in danger."

Three

OFFENSIVE STRATEGY

*G*enerally, in war the best policy is to take the enemy's country whole and intact; to ruin it is not so good. It is also better to capture the enemy's army than to destroy it; to take a regiment, a company or a five-man squad intact is better than to destroy them.

Fighting to win one hundred victories in one hundred battles is not the supreme skill. However to break the enemy's resistance without fighting is the supreme skill.

Thus, the general skilled in war places priority in attacking the enemy's strategy; the next best is to disrupt any alliances of the enemy; to be followed by the confrontation of his army.

The worst policy of all is to attack walled cities. Attack cities only as the last resort. The preparation of covered wagons, chariots and equipment requires three months; to pile up mounds against the walls shall take another three months.

"Fighting to win one hundred victories in one hundred battles is not the supreme skill. However to break the enemy's resistance without fighting is the supreme skill."

"A general is like
the spoke of a
wheel. If the
connection is
tight and
complete, the
wheel will be
strong and so will
be the State; if
the connection is
defective, then
the State will be
weak."

If the general cannot control his anger and sends his soldiers to swarm up the walls like ants, then one-third of the troops will be killed without taking the city. Such is the calamity of the attack.

The skilful general subdues the enemy's army without fighting. He captures cities without laying siege and overthrows the enemy's reign without protracted operations. Aim to take All-Under-Heaven intact. Thus, your troops are not wornout and your gains will be complete. This offensive strategy is that of 'using the sheathed sword'.

The way of fighting is: if our force is ten times the enemy's, then surround him; five times his, attack him; if double his strength, divide our force into two to be used as 'alternate strategy'; if only equal to his, we must concentrate our force to fight him.

When our casualties increase, withdraw. If our force is so much weaker than the enemy's, we should totally avoid him, for if a small army is stubborn, it will only end up being captured by the larger enemy force.

A general is like the spoke of a wheel. If the connection is tight and complete, the wheel will be strong and so will be the State; if the connection is defective, then the State will be weak.

There are three ways whereby a ruler can bring misfortune upon his army: By commanding an army to advance or retreat, when ignorant on whether to advance or retreat. This is called 'hobbling the army'.

By trying to administer an army the same way he administers a kingdom, when ignorant of military affairs. This causes the officers to be perplexed.

By using the army officers without discretion, when ignorant of the military principle of being flexible with the circumstances. This causes doubts in the minds of the officers. When the army is confused and suspicious, neighbouring rulers will surely cause trouble.

There are five circumstances in which victory may be predicted: He who knows when he can fight and when not to fight will be victorious. He who understands the use of both large and small forces will win. He whose ranks are united in purpose will be victorious. He who is prepared and lies in wait for an enemy who is not, will be victorious. He who has capable generals and without interference by the ruler will be victorious. It is in these five matters that the way to victory is known.

Therefore, I say: If you know yourself and know your enemy; in a hundred battles you will never fear the result. When you know yourself but not your enemy, your chances of winning or losing are equal. If you know neither yourself nor your enemy, you are certain to be in danger in every battle.

"If you know yourself and know your enemy; in a hundred battles you will never fear the result. When you know yourself but not your enemy, your chances of winning or losing are equal. If you know neither yourself nor your enemy, you are certain to be in danger in every battle."

Four

TACTICS

Skilful warriors of ancient times first sought for themselves an invincible position where they would await for the opportunity to strike at their enemy's vulnerability.

Invincibility lies in one's own hands, but the enemy's vulnerability is of his own making. Thus, those skilled in war can make themselves invincible but the enemy's vulnerability is provided only by the enemy himself.

Therefore, one may know how to win and yet is unable to do it. To be invincible, use defensive tactics; to make the enemy vulnerable, go on the offensive. Defend when one's strength is insufficient; attack when abundant.

Those skilled in defence appear to hide in the deepest nine-fold of the earth; those skilled in attack appear to move above the highest nine-fold of heaven. In this way, they can protect themselves and secure total victory.

To foresee a victory that others can also foresee is no great feat. There is no greatness in winning battles and being proclaimed universally

"Invincibility lies in one's own hands, but the enemy's vulnerability is of his own making. Thus, those skilled in war can make themselves invincible but the enemy's vulnerability is provided only by the enemy himself."

"What the ancients called a skilful fighter is one who not only wins but wins with ease.... He wins by making no mistakes. Making no mistakes means already having established the certainty of victory; conquering an enemy who is already defeated."

as an expert, for to lift a rabbit's hair requires no great strength; to see the sun and the moon is not a sign of sharp sight; to hear the thunderclap is not a sign of sharp hearing.

What the ancients called a skilful fighter is one who not only wins but wins with ease. But the victories will neither earn him a reputation for wisdom nor credit for valour. For victories are such, they are gained in circumstances that have not been revealed and he thus wins no reputation for wisdom; and as the enemy submits without bloodshed, he receives no credit for valour.

He wins by making no mistakes. Making no mistakes means already having established the certainty of victory; conquering an enemy who is already defeated.

Therefore, a skilful commander puts himself in a position secured against defeat and misses no opportunity to defeat his enemy. In this way, the victorious army seeks battle only after the victory has been secured; an army destined to defeat fights in the hope of winning.

The good commander seeks virtues and goes about disciplining himself according to the laws so as to effect control over his success.

There are five methods in the military art: first, measurement; second, calculation; third, quantification; fourth, comparison; and fifth, the possibility of winning.

Earth leads to measurement; measurement leads to calculation; calculation leads to quantification; quantification leads to comparison; comparison leads to the possibility of winning. The victorious army is as twenty-four taels against one-twentieth of a tael; while the defeated army is one-twentieth of a tael against twenty-four taels.

The onrushing of the victorious soldiers, like the pent-up waters of a huge dam suddenly released to plunge down a thousand feet deep valley, is power!

"Therefore, a skilful commander puts himself in a position secured against defeat and misses no opportunity to defeat his enemy."

Five

ENERGY

*M*anagement of many is the same as management of a few. It is a matter of dividing up their numbers and functions. Manoeuvering a large army is no different from manoeuvering a small one: it is a matter of formations and signals. In making sure the army can sustain the enemy's attack without suffering defeat, direct and indirect manoeuvres should be used.

Generally, in battle, use the direct methods to engage the enemy forces; indirect methods however are needed to secure victory.

In battle, there are only the direct or the indirect methods of fighting but they give an endless combination of manoeuvres. For both forces are interlocked and using each will lead to the other; it is like moving in a circle—you can never come to an end. Who can determine where one ends and the other begins?

Torrential water tosses stones along in its course due to its momentum. The well-timed swoop of a hawk enables it to strike its prey.

"Generally, in battle, use the direct methods to engage the enemy forces; indirect methods however are needed to secure victory."

"A skilled commander conserves energy from the situation instead of wasting his men. He selects his men according to their talents and uses them to exploit the situation."

Therefore, the momentum of one who is skilled in war would be overwhelming and his decision to strike is be well timed.

Energy is like a fully-drawn crossbow; the decision to strike is the timely release of the trigger.

Amid the turmoil and uproar of battle, the situation may appear to be chaotic and yet no real chaos exists; troops seem to be in disarray and yet cannot be routed. What is seen as confusion is actually good order; appearance of fear is in reality courage; appearance of weakness is yet true strength.

Order or disorder depends on organization; concealing valour for a cowardly front is on circumstances; masking strength with weakness is to be effected by tactical disposition.

Thus, the skilful general keeps the enemy on the move by maintaining deceitful appearances; he holds out something that the enemy is certain to go for, and with such baits keep the enemy going to where he lies in wait to strike.

A skilled commander conserves energy from the situation instead of wasting his men. He selects his men according to their talents and uses them to exploit the situation.

Hence, when he uses his men to fight, it is easy as moving logs and rocks. For it is the nature of logs and rocks to be static when the ground is stable; mobile when the ground is uneven, and immobile if in the square-shaped; rolling when round.

Thus, the energy generated in troops by a good commander, like the momentum of rolling a round boulder down a thousand feet high mountain, is powerful!

Six

WEAK AND STRONG POINTS

*T*he one who is first to occupy the battlefield to await the enemy will be fresh and at ease; he who comes later and rushes into the fight will be exhausted.

Therefore, the skilful commander imposes his will on the enemy by making the enemy come to him instead of being brought to the enemy.

To do this, he offers the enemy some advantages; and similarly, he is able to prevent the enemy's coming by inflicting damage on the enemy. When the enemy is taking his ease, harass him; when well supplied with food, attack his supply lines to starve him out; when he is at rest, force him to move. Appear at those places that he must hasten to defend; move swiftly to those where you are not expected.

That you may march a thousand *li* without exhaustion is due to the country being free of enemy troops. You can be sure of taking what you attack if you attack those places which are undefended. To ensure the safety of your posi-

"Therefore, the skilful commander imposes his will by making the enemy come to him instead of being brought to the enemy."

tion, hold only those positions that cannot be attacked.

For a general who is skilled in the offensive, the enemy would not know where to defend; and for one who is skilful in the defensive, the enemy would not know where to attack.

Subtle and secretive, the skilled learns to be invisible and silent to control the enemy's fate. He whose advances cannot be resisted makes for the enemy's weak areas; if there is need to withdraw, he moves so swiftly that he cannot be overtaken. When I wish to fight, my enemy who may be sheltered by high ramparts and deep moats, can be forced to come out into an engagement if I were to attack a position that he will be obliged to relieve.

When I wish to avoid a fight, I can prevent an engagement even though the battlelines had been drawn by diverting my enemy with something odd and unexpected thrown in his way.

By discovering my enemy's dispositions and at the same time concealing mine from him, I can concentrate my forces while he must divide his. Knowing his dispositions, I can pit my total strength against a part of his.

If he is ignorant of mine, he will have to spread out his forces to defend every point. This will give me superiority in numbers. And if I were to use my superior strength to attack an inferior one, those whom I deal with will be in dire straits.

The enemy must not know where I intend to attack. For when he does not know, he must prepare for possible attack in many places; and in such preparation, his forces shall be so spread out that those I have to fight with at any given point will be few.

Thus, when he prepares to defend the front, the rear will be weak; when he prepares to defend the rear, the front will weaken; similarly, left to right and right to left. If he prepares to defend everywhere, he will be weak everywhere.

One who has few must prepare for defence; one who has many shall make the enemy prepare for defence.

When we know the place and the date of the battle, then even for a thousand *li*, we can march forth to engage the enemy. But if we do not know where or when the enemy will attack, then our front and rear troops, left and right wings cannot protect each other. How much more then if our troops are distanced by a hundred li, or even short of a few *li*?

As I see it, even though the number of soldiers of Yue exceeds ours, can that help them win a battle? Thus, I can create victory. Even if the enemy is numerous, I can prevent him from fighting. Find out his plans and analyse which of his strategies will be successful and which will not. Provoke to agitate him and so learn the pattern of his movements. Force him to show his dispositions and thus ascertaining his strengths and weaknesses.

The supreme skill in commanding troops is in the shapeless command. Then, the prying of the subtlest spies cannot penetrate for the laying of plans against you.

The shapes I take shall lay plans for victory but such are beyond the comprehension of the masses. While all can see the external aspects,

"But if we do not know where or when the enemy will attack, then our front and rear troops, left and right wings cannot protect each other."

"Military tactics are similar to water, for just as flowing water runs away from high places and speeds downwards, so an army avoids the strong enemy and strikes at the weak one."

none can understand the way I scored my victory. Thus, when I win a victory, I do not repeat the tactics but respond to circumstances in limitless ways.

Military tactics are similar to water, for just as flowing water runs away from high places and speeds downwards, so an army avoids the strong enemy and strikes at the weak one. As water shapes its flow according to the ground, an army wins by relating to the enemy it faces. And just as water retains no constant shape, in war there will be no constant conditions.

Thus, he who can modify his tactics according to the enemy's situations shall be victorious and may be called The Divine Commander.

For none of the five elements—water, fire, wood, metal and earth—is always predominant; none of the four seasons can last forever; the days are sometimes longer and sometimes shorter; and the moon sometimes waxes and sometimes wanes.

Seven

MANOEUVRES

*W*ithout harmony in the State, no military expedition can be made; without harmony in the army, no battle formation can be directed. In war, the general first receives his commands from the ruler. He then assembles his troops and blends them into a harmonious entity before pitching camp.

Nothing is more difficult than directing manoeuvres. The difficulty lies in turning the devious into the direct, and misfortune into gain.

Thus, adopt an indirect route and divert the enemy by enticing him with a bait. Once done, you may march forth after he has gone and arrive before him. One who is able to do this knows the direct and indirect strategies. But while manoeuvres can offer advantages, they may also pose dangers.

When one sets in motion an entire army to chase an advantage, the chances are that he will not attain it.

If an army abandons the camp to fight for an advantage, it will have to give up heavy equip-

"Nothing is more difficult than directing manoeuvres. The difficulty lies in turning the devious into the direct, and misfortune into gain."

ment. Thus, in rolling up the armour to chase incessantly day and night, marching at double time for a hundred *li*, the commanders will only fall into the enemy's hands. This is because the stronger soldiers will arrive first while the feeble ones will fall behind, and by this method, only one-tenth of the troops will arrive.

In a forced march of fifty *li*, the front commander will fall and only half the troops will arrive. In a forced march of thirty *li*, then two-thirds will arrive.

An army cannot survive without its equipment, food and stores.

If we cannot fathom the designs of our neighbouring States, we cannot enter into alliances in advance.

Those who do not know the conditions of mountains, forests, high and dangerous grounds, defiles, marshes, and swamps cannot conduct the march of an army.

Those who do not use local guides cannot benefit from the advantages of the ground.

War is based on deception. Move only if there is a real advantage to be gained. Create changes in the situation by dividing or concentrating your forces.

Be swift as the wind, compact as the forest. In raiding and plundering, like fire; in stability, as the mountain. Let your plans be unfathomable as the clouds and your moves be like the thunderbolt.

When plundering the countryside and having captured new lands, divide the profits among your men. Always observe and assess the situation before making your move.

SUN TZU'S ART OF WAR

Winners are those who know the art of direct and indirect strategies. Such is the art of military manoeuvres.

According to the *Book of Military Administration*: "As orders cannot be heard clearly in the battlefield, so make use of bells and drums. As soldiers cannot distinguish each other in the confusing battle situation, so use flags and banners".

For drums and bells, flags and banners are to unify the sight and hearing of a person. When soldiers are thus united, the brave cannot advance alone and the coward also cannot withdraw. This is the art of controlling a large army.

Use torches and drums when fighting at night, and use flags and banners when fighting in the day-time, as means of influencing the enemy's sight and hearing.

An army may be robbed of its spirit and the commander be robbed of his wits. In the morning a soldier's spirit is keenness, during the day, it gradually diminishes, and in the evening, the soldier thinks only of returning to camp. Thus, the skilful commander avoids the enemy whose spirit is at its keenness and instead attacks only when the enemy's spirit is sluggish and thinking of camp. This is control of the spirit.

Prepare yourselves in good order to await a disorderly enemy; in calmness, await a boisterous one. This is control of the mind.

Close to the battlefield, await for the enemy coming from afar; at ease, await for a tired enemy; with well-fed troops, await for hungry ones. This is control of strength.

"Prepare yourselves in good order to await a disorderly enemy; in calmness, await a boisterous one....Close to the battlefield, await for the enemy coming from afar; at ease, await for a tired enemy; with well-fed troops, await for hungry ones."

"Do not pursue an enemy who pretends to flee. Refrain from attacking troops whose spirit is keen. Do not swallow baits put out by the enemy."

Do not engage an enemy whose banners are in perfect order or whose troops are arrayed in an impressive formation. This is control of circumstances.

Therefore, in accordance with military axioms, do not advance against the enemy who occupies higher ground; do not oppose him if he is coming downhill.

Do not pursue an enemy who pretends to flee. Refrain from attacking troops whose spirit is keen. Do not swallow baits put out by the enemy. Avoid stopping enemy troops on the home march. When surrounding an enemy, leave him an escape route. Do not press an enemy to desperation. This is the way of manoeuvering an army.

Eight

TACTICAL VARIATIONS

*I*n war, a general first receives commands from the ruler, then gathers the people, and assembles the troops.

Never encamp on swampy grounds.

Keep the ground for communication opened so that you may contact your allies.

Do not linger on grounds which are dangerously isolated. When trapped on grounds which are hemmed-in, use stratagem to break out. On death ground where desperation demands, then you must fight.

There are some roads which we must not follow; some enemy troops we must not fight; some cities we must not attack; some grounds we must not contest; even some orders from the ruler which we must not obey. A general who thoroughly understands the use of the nine variations, knows how to command an army.

A general who does not understand the nine variations, although familiar with the ground, will still be unable to take advantage of this familiarity.

"There are some roads which we must not follow; some enemy troops we must not fight; some cities we must not attack; some grounds we must not contest; even some orders from the ruler which we must not obey."

"It is a principle of war that we do not assume the enemy will not come, but instead we must be prepared for his coming; not to presume he will not attack, but instead make our own position unassailable."

In military operations, one who lacks the knowledge of the nine tactical variations, even if he has knowledge of the 'five advantages', will still be unable to use his troops effectively.

A wise general considers both the advantages and disadvantages opened to him. When considering the advantages, he makes his plan feasible; when considering the disadvantages, he finds ways to extricate himself from the difficulties.

Therefore, seek to reduce those *hostile* neighbouring States by bringing harm to them. Labour them with constant trifle affairs. Lead them by their noses with superficial offers of advantages.

It is a principle of war that we do not assume the enemy will not come, but instead we must be prepared for his coming; not to presume he will not attack, but instead make our own position unassailable.

There are five dangerous faults which a general should not have in his character. Recklessness, which leads to destruction; cowardice, which ends in capture; a quick temper, which enables you to make him look foolish; delicacy in honour, which causes sensitivity to shame; overly compassionate for his men, which exposes him to worry and harassment. These five faults in a general can seriously ruin military operations.

Nine

ON THE MARCH

*W*hen positioning an army to observe the enemy, cross over the mountains and stay close to the valleys. Position yourself on high ground with a wide view.

Never ascend to attack but only fight down-hill. This is mountain positioning.

After crossing a river, we must keep away from it. When the enemy crosses the river towards us, do not engage him in mid-stream. It will be advantageous to wait until half of the enemy troops are ashore, and then attack If we wish to fight, do not confront the enemy near the river. Choose a high position with a wide view. Never be positioned at downstream. This is river positioning.

Avoid swamps but if there is a need to cross them, do so quickly and without delay. If forced to fight in swamps, keep close to the grass and have the trees to your rear. This is positioning in swamps.

In level ground, choose a position easy to move on and easy to get your supplies. With

"When positioning an army to observe the enemy, cross over the mountains and stay close to the valleys. Position yourself on high ground with a wide view."

higher ground to the right and the rear, open plain in front and safety to the rear. This is positioning in level ground.

All these four methods of positioning armies were used by the Yellow Emperor when he conquered the four neighbouring countries.

An army prefers high ground to low; sunny places to cold and wet shady areas. Nourish your soldiers well and build up their internal strength so that they are free of hundreds of diseases, and this will ensure victory.

When near hills, mounds, embankments or dikes, take up the position that faces the sun and have higher ground to the right and rear. This is to benefit from the natural advantages of the ground.

When crossing a river with much bubbles in the water, this means that there were heavy rains at the upper stream, you should wait until the water subsides and calms down before crossing.

Whenever there are torrents—'Heavenly Wells', 'Heavenly Prisons', 'Heavenly Nets', 'Heavenly Traps' and 'Heavenly Gaps'—get away quickly. Do not go near them.

I keep away from them and lure the enemy towards them. I face the enemy and force him to put his back to them.

When on the march, there are dangerous defiles, swamps with aquatic grass and reeds, forests with dense tangled undergrowth, which must be carefully and repeatedly searched out, for these are the places where the enemy can lay ambushes or hide spies.

When the enemy is near but remains quiet, this means he is confidently relying on his impregnable position. When the enemy is far but keeps on challenging, he is trying to lure us to advance. If the enemy takes up a position that is easy for us to discover and attack, he could be offering an ostensible advantage to trap us. When there is movement amongst the trees, we know the enemy is advancing.

When obstacles are set up in the undergrowth, the enemy is seeking to deceive us. Birds that suddenly rise in flight show that there are men hiding in ambush positions; wild animals scurrying show the enemy is making surprise advances.

When dust rises in high columns, this shows that chariots are rushing forward; when dust is low and widespread, this means infantry is approaching.

When dust is scattered in different directions, the enemy is gathering firewood; when dust clouds are few and moving to and fro, the enemy is encamping his army.

When the enemy's envoys speak humbly but he is secretly preparing his force, he will advance. But when the language is fierce and the enemy threatens to attack, he is looking for a way to retreat.

When his chariots take up positions at both wings, he is ready to fight.

When without a previous understanding, the enemy presents peace proposals, he must be plotting against you.

"If the enemy takes up a position that is easy for us to discover and attack, he could be offering an ostensible advantage to trap us."

"When troops are seen whispering amongst themselves in small groups, the general has lost the confidence of his men. Too frequent rewards show that the general is losing control over his men.... Too frequent punishments show him to be in dire distress...."

When enemy troops are seen running about and getting into formations, then the 'expectant date' of attack as forewarned by the enemy's spies is drawing near.

When half his force is advancing and half is withdrawing, he is putting out a bait.

When his soldiers lean on their weapons, they are weakened by hunger.

When those sent to draw water rush to drink before carrying back to camp, the troops are suffering from water shortage.

When the enemy sees an advantage but makes no effort to advance and seize it, his army is exhausted.

When birds gather around the camp, it has been vacated. When soldiers shout loudly at night, they are nervous.

When the troops are in disorder, the general has lost his authority. When the flags and banners are shifted about, the army is in chaos. If the officers are short-tempered, it means that they are tired.

When the troops feed grain to their horses, slaughter the transport cattle for food, and do not hang up their cooking pots properly or do not return to their shelters, they are desperate and are preparing to fight to the death.

When troops are seen whispering amongst themselves in small groups, the general has lost the confidence of his men. Too frequent rewards show that the general is losing control over his men as only rewards can keep them in even temper. Too frequent punishments show him to be in dire distress as nothing else can keep them in check.

If the officers at first treat their men harshly and later fear them, then the limit of indiscipline is reached. When the enemy sends envoys to apologize, this shows he wants a truce.

When facing enemy troops who are in high spirits for some time without either joining battle or withdrawing, we must carefully analyse and observe the situation.

In battle, having more soldiers will not necessarily secure victory. Never advance by relying blindly on the strength of military power alone. It is sufficient to concentrate our strength, estimate the enemy's position and seek his capture. But anyone who lacks consideration and treats the enemy with contempt and disdain will only end up being captured himself.

Secure the loyalty of your troops first before punishing them or they will not be submissive. When they are loyal and if punishment is not enforced, you still cannot use them.

Therefore, treat your men kindly but keep strict control over them to ensure victory. If the commands used in training troops are consistent, soldiers will be disciplined. If not, soldiers are inclined to be disobedient. If a general's commands are consistently credible and obeyed, he enjoys good relationship with his men.

"Secure the loyalty of your troops first before punishing them or they will not be submissive. When they are loyal and if punishment is not enforced, you still cannot use them."

Ten

TERRAIN

*T*here are six types of ground befitting its nature: open, entangling, inconclusive, narrow, precipitous and distant.

Open ground is that which can be easily traversed by both sides. In such ground, we must occupy the higher position which faces the sun and is convenient for our supply routes so that we can fight with advantage.

It is easy to enter into entangling ground but difficult to withdraw from. In such ground, if the enemy is unprepared, our attack will certainly dislodge them. But if he is prepared and our attack fails to defeat him, then it would be difficult to retreat. This is the disadvantage of this ground.

Ground which is disadvantageous for both the enemy and ourselves is inconclusive ground. In such ground, do not advance to take the enemy's baits but instead seek to lure him forward by our retreat. Wait until half of his force has advanced, then attack to gain an advantage.

"Ground which is disadvantageous for both the enemy and ourselves is inconclusive ground. In such ground, do not advance to take the enemy's baits but instead seek to lure him forward by our retreat."

"When troops are inclined to flee, insubordinate against commands, distressed, disorganized or defeated, it is the fault of the general as none of these calamities arises from natural causes."

We must occupy narrow ground first, then block up the passes and await the enemy. If the enemy has already occupied it, follow him only if he has yet to block up the passes; if he has done so, then do not follow.

On precipitous ground, we must occupy the higher ground which faces the sun first and await the enemy. If the enemy has already occupied it, lure him to leave but never follow him in.

If we are at a distance from an enemy of equal strength, then it is difficult to engage him successfully.

These six grounds are the principles of Earth. It is the highest responsibility of a general to observe and study them.

When troops are inclined to flee, insubordinate against commands, distressed, disorganized or defeated, it is the fault of the general as none of these calamities arises from natural causes.

When other conditions are equal, if an army is outnumbered by ten to one, then the soldiers of the weaker force are certain to flee.

When the common soldiers are stronger than their officers, they will insubordinate.

When the officers are too strong and the troops are weak, the result is collapse.

When senior officers are angry and go against orders, and they fight on meeting the enemy without being told by their general whether such is feasible or not, the result is defeat.

When the general is morally weak and lacks authority; when his instructions are not clear; when there are no consistent rules to guide both officers and men, and the ranks are slovenly formed, the result is disorganization.

When a general fails to size up his enemy and uses an inferior force to engage a larger one, or weak troops to attack the strong, or neglects to place picked men in the front ranks, the result is a rout.

These six conditions shall lead to failure. It is also the highest responsibility of a general to study them carefully.

Conformation of the terrain is the soldier's best ally in battle. Thus, victory rests with the superior general who can size up his enemy and provide for the distances in travel and the nature of the land with all its difficulties. He who understands this principle and uses it to conduct the fight will certainly win; he who does not will fail.

If the situation offers victory but the ruler forbids fighting, the general may still fight. If the situation is such that he cannot win, then the general must not fight even if the ruler orders him to do so.

Thus, the general who advances without coveting fame and withdraws without fearing disgrace, but whose sole intention is to protect the people and do good service for his ruler, is the precious jewel of the State.

Such a general who protects his soldiers like infants will have them following him into the deepest valleys. A general who treats his soldiers like his own beloved sons will have their willingness to die with him.

However, if he is too indulgent; if he loves them too much to enforce his commands; and

"Thus, the general who advances without coveting fame and withdraws without fearing disgrace, but whose sole intention is to protect the people and do good service for his ruler, is the precious jewel of the State."

cannot assert control when the troops are in disorder, then the soldiers are similar to spoilt children and shall became useless.

If I know my soldiers are capable of attacking the enemy but am unaware that he is invulnerable to attack, my chance of victory is but half.

If I know the enemy is open to attack but do not know my soldiers are incapable of attacking him, my chance of victory is but half.

If I know the enemy can be attacked and my soldiers are capable of doing it but am unaware that the terrain is unsuited for fighting, I should hold back for my chance of victory is but half.

Thus, when those skilled in war make their move, there is no mistake; when they act, they have unlimited resources. So I say: Know your enemy, know yourself and your victory will be undoubted. Know Earth, know Heaven and your victory will be complete.

Eleven

THE NINE VARIETIES
OF GROUND

*I*n commanding an army, classify ground into nine varieties; dispersive, frontier, key, open, intersecting, vital, difficult, enclosed, and death.

When a feudal lord fights in his own territory, he is on dispersive ground.

When he penetrates slightly into the territory of others, he is on frontier ground.

Ground that gives advantage to any warring party is key ground.

Ground that is accessible by both the warring parties is open ground.

The ground that is enclosed by three States and whoever is first in occupying it will gain the support of All-Under-Heaven is intersecting ground.

When an army has advanced deep into the enemy's territory, leaving many enemy cities and towns behind, it is vital ground.

When an army marches through mountains, forests, precipitous land, swamps, or any place that is dangerous to march, it is moving on difficult ground.

"We move when there is advantage to gain; we halt when there is none."

Ground that has a narrow access and tortuous exit, whereby the smaller enemy force can crush my larger one, is enclosed ground.

Ground in which only a desperate fight may offer survival is death ground.

Therefore, do not fight on dispersive ground; do not halt on frontier ground; do not attack an enemy who has already occupied key ground; do not break up our formations into separate units on open ground.

Form alliances with neighbouring States on intersecting ground; plunder when on vital ground.

On difficult ground, keep moving; on enclosed ground, use strategies; on death ground, fight.

Those skilful commanders of old knew how to split the enemy's unity between the front and rear troops; to prevent co-operation between the main force and the reinforcement; to hinder the stronger troops from rescuing the weaker ones, and subordinates from supporting their superiors.

Disperse the enemy troops and prevent them from assembling; even though his soldiers are gathered, they will be in disorder.

We move when there is advantage to gain; we halt when there is none.

Should one ask: "If attacked by a large and orderly enemy troops, what shall I do?" I would reply: "Seize something that he holds dear so that he has no choice but to yield to your will." Speed is the essence of war. Take advantage of the enemy's lack of preparation; move by using unexpected routes and attack where he has made no defence.

When we are deep in the enemy's territory, be 'the guest of our enemy'; the deeper we penetrate, the more united will our soldiers be and thus, the enemy cannot overcome us.

Plunder the fertile countryside to get enough food for our army.

Give attention to the well-being of your men; do not exhaust them unnecessarily. Keep their spirit united; conserve their energy.

Do not let your enemy understand the plans concerning your troops' movements. Put your men in positions where there is no escape and even when facing death, they will not run. In preparing for death, what is there that cannot be achieved? Both officers and men will do their best. In a desperate situation, they lose their sense of fear; without a way out, they shall stand firm. When they are deep within the enemy's territory they are bound together and without an alternative, they will fight hard.

Thus, without need of supervision, they will be alert, and without being asked, they will support their general; without being ordered, they will trust him.

If my officers are not exceedingly rich, it is not that they disdain wealth. If they do not expect long life, it is not because of their dislike for longevity.

On the day the army is ordered to march, soldiers who are seated will cry till their lapels are soaked; the tears of those who are reclining will wet their cheeks. But once they are thrown into battle where there is no escape, they will show incredible courage like that of Chuan Chu and Ts'ao Kuei.

"Give attention to the well-being of your men; do not exhaust them unnecessarily. Keep their spirit united; conserve their energy."

Thus, a good general commands the army like the *shuai-ran*, a huge snake found in the Ch'ang mountains. When struck on the head, its tail attacks; when struck on the tail, its head attacks; when struck in the middle, both head and tail attack.

Should someone ask: "Can an army be commanded like the *shuai-ran?*", I would answer: "Yes." The people of Wu and Yue mutually hate each other but when they sail in the same boat tossed by the wind, they will help each other just like the right hand co-operates with the left.

Therefore, the burying of wheels deep into the soil to stabilize the chariot or the tethering of the war horses is not sufficient to place one's dependance upon.

In military administration, cultivate a uniform level of courage. Make use of the advantage of the ground so as to bring out the best of both strong and weak soldiers. A wise general thus leads the entire army like he is leading one person. It is the business of a general to be calm and mysterious; fair and composed. He must be capable of mystifying his officers and men so that they are ignorant of his true intentions.

He forbids the casting of omens and do away with superstitious beliefs that even until the time of death, no calamity need be feared.

He changes his arrangements and alters his plans so that no one knows what he is up to. He changes campsites and takes circuitous routes to prevent others from anticipating his purpose.

He leads the army into battle just like a person who has climbed to the heights and then kicks away the ladder behind him so as to put them into a desperate position. His business is to assemble his troops and throw them into a critical position. He leads them deep into enemy's territory to further his plans. He burns the boats and breaks the cooking pots; like one shepherding a flock of sheep, he drives the army here and there, and none knows where he is going.

The changes of the nine varieties of ground gives varying advantages of attacking and defending; and the behaviour of the soldiers are matters which must be studied seriously.

When your army advances into the enemy's territory, then 'be his guest' and if our penetration is deep and your soldiers know there is no turning back, they will concentrate their fighting spirit. If your penetration is shallow and soldiers are still thinking of home, their spirit will be distracted.

After leaving your own country, march your army across the border and you are in frontier ground. When there are convergences of all roads from different directions, that is known as open ground.

When you have penetrated deeply into the enemy's territory, that is vital ground. Shallow penetration is frontier ground. When the enemy's force is solidly to your rear and you face a narrow pass in front, you are now on enclosed ground.

A place with no way to turn to is death ground. Therefore, when in dispersive ground, I will unify the soldiers' fighting spirit; in frontier ground, I will make sure that our troops are

"The changes of the nine varieties of ground gives varying advantages of attacking and defending; and the behaviour of the soldiers are matters which must be studied seriously."

well linked up. On key ground, I will rush up our rear troops; on open ground, I will increase our vigilance.

On intersecting ground, I will strengthen my alliance; On vital ground, I will make sure continued provisions are safeguarded; on difficult ground, I will push the army to march on; on enclosed ground, I will block the passes; on death ground, I will show the soldiers that there is no other way to survive but to fight.

For the nature of soldiers is such that when surrounded, will defend; when desperate, will fight; when in peril, will obey promptly.

If we cannot fathom the designs of our neighbouring States, we cannot enter into alliances in advance. Those who do not know the conditions of mountains, forests, high and dangerous grounds, defiles, marshes, and swamps cannot conduct the march of an army. Those who do not use local guides cannot benefit from the advantages of the ground.

To be ignorant of the nine varieties of ground is not befitting the command of the army of the Supreme King.

When the army of the Supreme King attacks a large State, the latter shall be unable to concentrate its forces. Being thus intimidated by its might, the allies of the large State will not dare come to its aid.

There is neither the need to fight the combined States nor is there any need to foster the power of the other States. The Supreme King's army can rely on its own ability to overawe its enemies. It can thus conquer their cities and destroy their kingdoms.

Bestow rewards without regard to customary rules, issue orders without regard to prescribed procedures. Thus, you may run the entire army as you would one man.

Assign tasks to your soldiers without detailing your plan. Show them the advantages without revealing the dangers. Put your men into a perilous spot and they will survive; trap them on death ground and they will fight for their lives. For only when the army is in danger that they can turn defeat into victory.

To be successful in warfare, we must pretend we are keeping to the enemy's designs. Concentrate your forces against his and then you can kill his general from a thousand *li* away. This is called achieving your task in a tricky and artful way.

On the day of commencing the attack, seal off the passes, cancel all passports, have no more contact with the enemy's envoys, speak seriously in the temple on the decision for the battle.

Whenever the enemy presents an opportunity, take it quickly. Anticipate him by seizing what he holds dear, check the situation of his force, and secretly fix a day to launch the attack.

Therefore, at the start of the battle, be as coy as a virgin; when your enemy lowers his guard and offers an opening, rush in like a hare out of its cage and the enemy will be unable to defend in time.

"Bestow rewards without regard to customary rules, issue orders without regard to prescribed procedures."

Twelve

ATTACK BY FIRE

T here are five methods of attacking with fire. First, burning soldiers in their camp or towns; second, burning down stores; third, burning of transportation; fourth, burning down arsenals; and the fifth, firing torched arrows into the enemy's camp to create chaos and disorder.

There must be a good reason for using fire and the equipment to be used must be prepared well and readily available.

The weather and timing must be right when attacking with fire. Dry weather is essential. The timing should be when the moon is at the following positions: 'star of the green dragon' (eastern); 'star of martial enigma' (northern); 'star of the white tiger' (western); and 'star of the red sparrow' (southern). For these are the days of rising wind.

To attack by fire, we should respond differently according to the five methods of attack.

If fire is started in the enemy's camp by our undercover spies, we should respond by attacking immediately. When fire breaks out but his

"Therefore, to win battles and make conquests and to take over all the subjects, but failing to rebuild or restore the welfare of what one gained would be a bad omen..."

"Do not use your troops unless you can win. Do not fight unless you are in danger. No ruler should put troops into the field because he is angry; no general should fight because he is resentful."

soldiers remain calm, then instead of rushing in we must hold back from attacking for there must be some ruse afoot.

When the fire burns to an uncontrollable inferno, follow up with an attack if the situation allows; otherwise, wait.

The right weather and timing can allow you to trigger off the fire attack from without instead of from within. Set fire according to the direction of the wind, not against it.

Generally, when it is windy the whole day, the night will be calm; observe this accurately.

All armies must possess knowledge of these five different methods of attacking with fire. Always keep vigilance of the weather and the enemy's condition.

Thus, to attack by fire is intelligent for its effect is instantaneous and obvious.

Attack with water only on the condition we have a very strong army, for water can result in isolating the enemy's troops but it cannot destroy his supplies or equipment, thus it is not so effective.

Therefore, to win battles and make conquests and to take over all the subjects, but failing to rebuild or restore the welfare of what one gained would be a bad omen—it is considered as or so called 'wasteful stay'.

The enlightened ruler plans well ahead, and good generals serve to execute the plans.

Do not act unless it is in the interest of the State. Do not use your troops unless you can win. Do not fight unless you are in danger.

No ruler should put troops into the field because he is angry; no general should fight because he is resentful. Move when there is benefit to be gained, quit when there is no more advantage. For an angry man can later become happy, a resentful man become pleased, but a kingdom once destroyed can never be restored nor the dead be brought back to life.

Hence the enlightened ruler is prudent and the good general should not be hasty. Thus a country is safe and the army preserved.

"...an angry man can later become happy, a resentful man become pleased, but a kingdom once destroyed can never be restored nor the dead be brought back to life.

Thirteen

ESPIONAGE

*T*o raise an army of a hundred thousand soldiers and march them a thousand *li* to battle entails a heavy burden on both the people and the State's treasury, as expenses can amount to a thousand pieces of gold a day. There will be chaos at home and abroad; both soldiers and civilians will be exhausted on the routes causing the affairs of seven-hundred thousand households to be abandoned.

He who faces an enemy for many years, to struggle for the victory that can be decided in a single day and yet remains ignorant of the enemy's position because he begrudges giving ranks, honours and a few hundred pieces of gold [to spies or informants], is totally without humanity. Such a man is no leader, no help to his ruler, no master of victory.

The enlightened ruler and the wise general can subdue the enemy whenever they move and they can achieve superhuman feats because they have foreknowledge. This foreknowledge cannot be obtained from the spirits, gods, or by

"The enlightened ruler and the wise general can subdue the enemy whenever they move and they can achieve superhuman feats because they have foreknowledge."

reasoning over past events, or by calculations. It can only be obtained from men who know the enemy's position.

There are five classes of spies: native spies, inside spies, converted spies, condemned spies, and surviving spies.

When these five classes of spies are all at work simultaneously and none can penetrate their operations, they are called the "spiritual and mystic web of threads" and are the treasures of a ruler.

Native spies are those living in the enemy's country whom we employ as suppliers of reliable information.

Inside spies are those dissatisfied enemy officials whom we bribe for valuable information.

Converted spies are really the enemy's spies whom we feed with false information or make use of to spread rumours so as to lure the enemy into our traps.

Condemned spies are our spies who shall pretend to turn traitors so as to supply false information to the enemy, or our spies who have been deliberately fed with false information and then shall suffer capture by the enemy. They will certainly be executed when the enemy realizes the deceit.

Surviving spies are our spies who are selected for extremely tough and high-intelligence undercover missions within the enemy's territory. They are expected to make use of all means to learn and collect information before sneaking back to report.

The relationship between the commander and his secret agent is more intimate than all others in the army. The rewards given to secret agents are more liberal than any other given. The confidentiality given to secret operations is greater than for other matters. Only the one who is wise and sagely, benevolent and just, can use secret agents. Only he who is sensitive and subtle can get the truth of their reports. Be subtle, be subtle, and you can use espionage anywhere. Subtle, and most delicate, there are no means that cannot be used in espionage.

If the secret mission leaks out before an operation, then the spy and those whom he has spoken to should all be put to death.

Whichever army you wish to attack, city you wish to conquer, or person whom you wish to assassinate, you must know the names of the commanders, chief assistants, bodyguards, sentries and other subordinates, so make your spies check and acquire these facts accurately.

It is important to find out who are those sent by the enemy to spy on you and bribe them to serve you instead. Tempt them with bribes and house them well. This way you not only convert them for your use but also get to recruit other agents living in the enemy's land or working for the enemy. It is also in this manner that condemned spies, fed with false informations can be sent to cheat enemy. By this way too surviving spies can be sent to accomplish their tasks and return in due time.

A ruler should have total understanding about the activities of the five classes of spies. This knowledge comes mostly from converted spies and they must be treated with great im-

"It is important to find out who are those sent by the enemy to spy on you...."

"Espionage is vital in war because the army's ability to make the correct moves depends on it."

portance. In ancient times, when Yin succeeded Hsia in power, it was due to I-Chih who as the chief minister of Hsia was responsible for the State's affairs; then, when Chou succeeded Yin, it was Lu Ya, the former Minister of Yin, who helped Chou to construct the solid foundation for a glorious dynasty of twenty-nine generations. Hence only the enlightened ruler and the wise general who are capable of using intelligent people as spies, can achieve great things. Espionage is vital in war because the army's ability to make the correct moves depends on it.

W<u>SUN TZU'S ART OF WAR</u>K
W AR AT WOR K

**Applying
Sun Tzu's *Art Of War*
in today's business world.**

WAR AT WORK shows how the principles in Sun Tzu's *Art Of War* can be applied to resolve the various problems of the business world today—keeping ahead of rivals, devising strategies to ensure competitiveness, making accurate decisions under tremendous pressure, mobilizing resources, motivating the workforce, and the like.

The author, who has successfully tried and tested Sun Tzu's teachings in the training of his managers, interprets them lucidly and then explains in layman's language how to 'fight it out' in the modern business and corporate battlefields with the aim of improving profitability, productivity, working environment, and interpersonal relationships.

The ideas presented in *WAR AT WORK* will be extremely useful and relevant not only to businessmen, executives, managers, and administrators but also to anyone seeking ways to improve their performance in the workplace—and eventually derive greater satisfaction in their personal lives too.

Khoo Kheng-Hor

ISBN 967 978 340 5

Sun Tzu & Management

According to Khoo Kheng-Hor, managers seeking success must work towards controlling themselves as well as both the internal and external environments. One must look within oneself as the starting point in developing awareness of one's strengths and weaknesses. One must then view one's immediate environment and learn to cope with office politicking and other corporate power games. One must learn the relevance of Sun Tzu's principles in formulating and implementing strategies in the increasingly competitive world of business. This book also explains how the Japanese have benefited from Sun Tzu's *Art Of War* to become the world's leading economic power today.

Despite Sun Tzu's archaic fondness for grandiose expressions, his advice on timing, maneuvring, flexibility, and complete knowledge of the the enemy's strengths and weaknesses remains as powerful today as when it was first written approximately 2,500 years ago. *SUN TZU & MANAGEMENT* is a practical book designed to be enjoyed and to fill a gap in management literature.

It covers what should be familiar ground and is based entirely on real-life situations and observations. It will undoubtedly provoke thought and will stimulate managers to assess their own performance and to take positive steps to become more effective in their workplace.

Khoo Kheng-Hor

ISBN 967 978 424 X